Runes for Beginners

A Guide to Understanding and Using the Ancient Germanic Alphabet

Sebastian Berg

The work contained herein has been produced with the intent to provide relevant knowledge and information on the topic on the topic described in the title for entertainment purposes only. While the author has gone to every extent to furnish up to date and true information, no claims can be made as to its accuracy or validity as the author has made no claims to be an expert on this topic. Notwithstanding, the reader is asked to do their own research and consult any subject matter experts they deem necessary to ensure the quality and accuracy of the material presented herein.

This statement is legally binding as deemed by the Committee of Publishers Association and the American Bar Association for the territory of the United States. Other jurisdictions may apply their own legal statutes. Any reproduction, transmission or copying of this material contained in this work without the express written consent of the copyright holder shall be deemed as a copyright violation as per the current legislation in force on the date of publishing and subsequent time thereafter. All additional works derived from this material may be claimed by the holder of this copyright.

The data, depictions, events, descriptions and all other information forthwith are considered to be true, fair and accurate unless the work is expressly described as a work of fiction. Regardless of the nature of this work, the Publisher is exempt from any responsibility of actions taken by the reader in conjunction with this work. The Publisher acknowledges that the reader acts of their own accord and releases the author and Publisher of any responsibility for the observance of tips, advice, counsel, strategies and techniques that may be offered in this volume.

Table of Contents

Introduction

I would like to thank you for choosing this book, and I hope that it serves you well as a guideline for runes. Runes have been around for many, many years. They have been around so long, in fact, that we aren't really sure when they came to be. It is safe to say, though, that for the Nordic people, runes have always been in their life.

We will start by talking about the history of the runes, which we don't have a lot of information we are certain about, but we can get a good idea of how they came to be. It also goes a long way in showing their importance to the Nordic people and why they are a great magical tool.

Then we will discuss the runes themselves. This is going to be the bulk of the information in this book because we will go over every single rune in the Elder Futhark and their meaning.

The Elder Futhark will be broken down into its three aettir, which are Freyr's, Hagal's, and Tyr's Aett. Each section will hold eight runes to create a grand total of 24 runes.

After that will look at how to use runes in divination and magic. This is likely what has brought you here today because rune divination is very popular among people who already do tarot, or who is afraid to have to memorize the meanings of all the tarot cards. Since there are only 24 runes, it's a lot easier to remember their meanings and interpret readings.

So let's get started.

Chapter 1:

What Are Runes

Most runologists like to argue about the details of the history of runes, but there is an agreement about the general outline. Runes were thought to have been created from some of the Old Italic alphabets that were used by the Mediterranean people who lived in the first century CE. They lived south of the Germanic tribes. Early Germanic symbols like those that were preserved in rock carvings in northern Europe helped to develop the script.

The earliest runic inscription was found on a Meldorf brooch that was created in northern Germany about 50 CE. It was a very ambiguous inscription, and scholars have been split over whether the letters are Roman, runic, or a combination of both. The first clear inscriptions were found on the Ovre Stabu spearhead found in southern Norway and the Vimose comb out of Vimose, Denmark; both of these dates back to about 160 CE. The Kylver stone in Gotland holds one of the earliest carvings of the whole Futhark in the correct order. It has been dated to around 400 CE.

Their switch up with writing, from southern to northern Europe, was caused by Germanic warbands who encountered Italic writing during wars against their neighbors to the south. This is also supported by the theory that the runes were associated with Odin. He was the god of war and the patron of all of the war activities. Tacitus, the Roman historian, had explained that Odin was the main god within the pantheon of most of the German tribes during the first century. It isn't clear if the cult of Odin and the runes rose up together or if the latter came before the first doesn't really matter.

The way ancient Germanic people perceive the runes is that they don't come from a source that was as mundane as the Old Italic alphabet. They did not invent the runes, but pre-existed and eternal forced that Odin found by dealing with his harrowing ordeal. This story comes from an Old Norse poem called *Havamal* or *The Sayings of the High One*:

"I know that I hung on the wind-blasted tree all of the nights nine, pierced by my spear and given to Odin, myself sacrificed to myself on that pole of which none know where its roots run."

"No aid I received, not even a sip from the horn. Peering down, I took up the runes – screaming, I grasped them – then I fell back from there."

The tree that Odin hung himself from is said to have been Yggdrasil, which is the world tree found in the middle of the Germanic cosmos. Yggdrasil's roots and branches hold up the Nine Worlds. Right under this tree is the Well or Urd, where you will find a lot of wisdom. The runes have their own dwelling place in the water. This can be seen in a different Old Norse poem called the *Voluspa* or *Insight of the Seeress*:

"There stands an ash called Yggdrasil; a might tree showered in white hail. From there come the dews that fall in the valleys. It stands evergreen above Urd's Well."

"From there come maidens, very wise, three from the lake that stands beneath the pole. Once is called Urd, another Verdandi, Skuld the third; they carve into the tree the lives and fates of children."

The three maidens that the poem talks about are the Norns and the carvings that were on the runes. This has provided and a clear connection between the runes and the Urd or Well, as well as magic. The magic in them comes from the Norn's ability to carve the fate of every being.

Once Odin discovered the runes through his self-sacrifice and spent nine days fasting as he stared into the Well of Urd, he then gave the runes to the very first runemaster. His sacrifice was imitated symbolically in ceremonies where candidates learned about the history of the runes. There isn't any concrete evidence about this practice that has survived over the years.

Development and Origins

The actual origins of the runic alphabet are shrouded in a lot of mystery. The earliest inscription is the one that reads Harja that might mean warrior or comb, which can be found on the Vimose comb in Denmark that dates back to 160 CE. This uses the runes so maturely and confidently that scholars think it resulted from about 100 years' experience from writing the runes over this amount of time.

How this tradition was created has been debated and speculated for many years. Inspirations from the Roman and Greek alphabet, along with Danish and Italic origins have been suggested. The most likely is the Greek since it does resemble a variation of the Greek alphabet. The Greek alphabet was unstandardized between the years of 700 to 400 BCE. It could have reached Germanic speakers through groups that were made up of eastern Europeans. The mythology of the Norse gives us the story of Odin and his sacrifice.

Whichever one you want to believe in, by 500 CE, the use of runes was being done all across Germany from England, Denmark, Sweden, and Norway and to outposts in Hungary, Poland, Russia, and Germany and was recorded in different German languages. The main runic alphabets that were known were:

- Elder Futhark from 160 to 700 CE
- Younger Futhark from 700 to 1200 CE
- Anglo-Saxon Futhorc from the fifth century to 1000 CE

- Medieval Futhark which was formed in the 13th century CE

From the earliest remains that have been found that shows the runic alphabet isn't an actual language but was used in different texts to write many different German languages that were spoken across a huge geographic area. The shapes of the runes might vary along with layout, medium, usage, and order, which results in chronological, social, and regional differences. There isn't a standardized runic alphabet. All the variations were created by 700 CE, which can be seen by the uniform Elder Futhark to the smaller Younger Futhark from Scandinavia that would later change into Medieval Futhark and then the elaborate Anglo-Saxon Futhorc found across Frisia and Britain.

There are various theories about who created the runes, and some of these do have more supporters than others do, but all of them have something in common. Not one of these theories can be 100 percent proven. No runic alphabet can be truthfully dated to before 200 AD.

I have chosen to follow the theory that they were created between 100 and 200 AD among the

Germanic tribes that were located near the Black Sea. Runes could have been inspired by the Latin and Greek alphabets. Many will argue over this theory. Later the runes would be spread across the middle and north part of Europe by these tribes migrating.

Runes were first used by the Frisians, Germans, Herules, and Goths in the middle and south of Europe and by the Saxons and Angles toward the west. They were used by the Danish, Swedish, and Norwegian to the north. They were also used by the Sami of Lapland and by the people from Greenland and Iceland.

In Scandinavia, the runic alphabet was the only one used by 300 AD. It stopped being used because the Latin alphabet became popular in middle Europe; this was caused by Christianity being expanded into that region.

One has the ability to write runes from right to left of left to right. They could be written with the first sentence going from right to left and the second sentence going from left to right. Plus, runes were written bound together, upside down, or as a mirror image. Once rune could represent two runes like the rune, "FE" could show "FE + FE."

The runes were sometimes written as a continuous line of text without spaces between sentences or words. If the runemaster wanted to separate sentences or words, they would use a notation that looked like the letter "X" or with up to three points put over each other. If they used two points, that sentence might look something like: "I:MAKE:SPACE:WITH:TWO:POINTS."

You won't find any lowercase runes as they only came in uppercase.

There aren't any limits on the format that the runes are written in. Runes can be written in all sorts of directions and on any type of material. They could be magical formulas, hidden, or beautiful decorations. When the runes were carved into stone, they were made by carving many points close together until they have formed a line.

Four Theories

1. Turgay Kurum

Turgay Kurum from Turkey states that he wrote an article to catch his readers' attention to the Futhark alphabet and the fact that it is from the same origin as the ancient Gokturk alphabet that the Turkis inscriptions were written in.

2. Crete – 1800 to 400 BC

Runes were introduced into Scandinavia at the same time the spiral ornaments were introduced from Crete, which was around 1800 to 400 BC. If you look at this theory, the Goths were familiar with the runes before they even left Scandinavia, which was between 200 BE and 200 AD. This is not a well-known theory.

3. South Scandinavia – 300 AD

The runes that were made in South Scandinavia during 300 AD. The Latin alphabet gave them the inspiration for this, but they put it in relation to the Scandinavian culture. South Scandinavia was the epic center for runes during ancient times.

4. Latin or Greek Alphabet Inspiration

Kjell Aartun, who is a language researcher and doctor of philosophy, wrote that he proved the runes weren't inspired by the Latin or Greek alphabets. He says it is the complete opposite and states the Norwegian runes are the same as the runes used in Semitic languages like Canaan and Trojan Asia Minor that dates back to 2000 BC.

In his opinion, the runes are just one of several oriental writings that were the platform for the Latin and Greek alphabets when they were created later. He also writes that he is able to prove the first Norweigan runic inscriptions were written in Semitic languages. He cites cult based erotic texts that include the act of lovemaking.

He claims that new archeological finds indicated many people who lived near the Mediterranean Sea, would travel to the north on trading expeditions, especially the Cretans. During the Migration Period, people who spoke Semitic traveled to Norway. He says he came to this conclusion from facts that state: "the Asians in the north part of Asia spread so quickly that their language was common throughout all those countries."

Aartun's theories haven't been accepted by Norwegian runologists. His theory does have some online supporters.

Chapter 2:

The Elder Futhark

With a decent understanding of the history of runes, we can move on and learn their meanings and what makes them so powerful. The Elder Futhark is believed to be the most ancient Germanic runic alphabet. It got its name Futhark from the first six runes of the alphabet: Fehu, Uruz, Thurisaz, Ansuz, Raidho, and Kaunaz. This is similar to how the Greek word alphabet was created using the first two Greek letters, Alpha and Beta. As mentioned in the introduction, the Elder Futhark is broken down into three sections of eight runes. We'll begin with Freyr's Aett.

Freyr's Aett

ᚠ Fehu

The first letter is Fehu, which is pronounced "Fay-who." Its literal translation is "cattle."

Psychologically, it represents young love, first impressions, freedom, presence, and beginner's mind. Its energy shows sexual attraction, circulation, abundance, liquid and mobile transferable energies, dynamic power, charisma, luck, and mobility.

When Fehu appears in a divination reading, it often represents control, money, travel, energy, foresight, social success, and new beginnings. When reversed, it could mean endings, poverty, atrophy, failure, or greed.

Fehu is considered to be the rune of luck. Chance is not what makes the world go round; luck does. Luck is hidden, but it is very much an energy field that lives within all of us. Fehu controls your ability to hold onto your luck and to use it. All of the accumulated luck you have is your basic energy and acts as the foundation of your power and wealth in life. Performing courageous acts are central to being able to improve your "luck."

When beginning new things, Fehu will active your will, assist in goal-setting, and restore self-confidence, which is followed by immediate action.

You should use this symbol and what it teaches to fight procrastination. It reminds you to think for yourself, which is a fundamental practice to working with runes. Fehu's vibration is often connected to the basics of sexual attraction, young love, and a first impression. Fehu reminds us that we should act out of the present moment.

Consciously using money to live is central to Fehu. In our society, it's extremely important to look at new definitions of what wealth is and realize what is truly valuable. Wealth is creative and not a measurable or static mass.

ᚢ Uruz

The second letter is Uruz, pronounced "oo-ruse." Its literal translation is "Aurochs."

Its energy is organic structuring, manifestation, endurance, healing, survival, raw primal power, archetypal patterning, and vital formative force.

When it appears in a divination reading, it could mean understanding, pragmatic knowledge, health, luck, pattern, tenacity, vitality, constancy, and strength. If it is reversed, it could mean brutality, insensitivity, uncontrolled rage, ignorance, sickness, inconstancy, misdirected force, obsession, or weakness.

While Fehu symbolizes domesticated cattle, Uruz symbolizes the wild bovine. This serves as a reminder that cattle use to be wild creatures. While Fehu is represented by young lovers, Uruz represents that young warrior.

Life's persistent and resourceful will of survival is implicit within Uruz and is a rune of manifestation, endurance, and regeneration. Uruz energy pattern helps the ego and can protect the psyche. Its self-healing energy can help to pull an illness or disease back into its "primal blueprint," which is what its original shape was supposed to be.

This is the rune of your inner Queen and King. We are able to stand up for our rights and be free in the same type of authority that aurochs did. This shows the universe you have the will to live free and passionate.

ᚦ Thurisaz

Next up is Thurisaz, pronounced "Thor-is-as." It literally translates to "Thurses" or "Giants."

Psychologically it represents male sexual prowess, struggles against unconsciousness, and enthusiasm. Its energy is destructive storms, breaker of resistance, active defensive force, chaos, self-empowerment, and enthusiasm.

When Thurisaz appears in a divination reading, it means constructive conflict, regenerative catalyst, vital eroticism, directed forced, or reactive force. When it appears reversed, it means strife, annoyance, explosive violence, disease, dullness, betrayal, compulsion, defenselessness, or danger

It is common for Thurisaz to be described as something sharp, evil, a thorn, or grim. However, it represents Thor and his hammer, who protects Asgard from all of the giants who do not want to accept consciousness through the multiverse. In all respects, the energy of Thurisaz is forceful, brute violence, and ignorance. Thurisaz shows us the warrior that has wisdom and consciousness even when they need to use force. Thor represents those who are free and courageous and is the ultimate fighting force.

It is also considered a fertility rune because it can help you to get rid of the barren, rocky realm and work it into a fruitfulness womb. One of the best mentalities for working with this rune is enthusiasm and not fear or anger since the former will help you with awareness and will get rid of the possible danger of facing the magic of Thurisaz.

ᚨ Ansuz

The next rune is Ansuz, pronounced "Anne-suhz." Its literal translation is "Woden."

Psychologically is represents listening, inspiration, communion, and mental stability. Its energy is answers, order, exploration, communication, breath, animating spirit, and sovereign ancestral god.

When Ansuz appears in divination, it means open paths of communication, intellect, transformation, synthesis, word-power, or divine inspiration. When reversed, it could mean bad advice, boredom, manipulation by others, delusion, or misunderstanding.

The first gift to humans that Odin gave them was the breath of life and inspired mental activity, as well as cognitive senses, form, and speech. The main energy of Ansuz triggers ecstatic mental states and inspiration. Our mind's ability to work with patterns is inherent in the energy of Ansuz.

The spirit becomes one with the body as soon as the baby breathes its first breath. It will only leave once the person takes its last breath. Breath is where osmosis between the physical world and the transpersonal energy happens. Meditation helps emphasize the breath.

ᚱ Raidho

Next up is Raidho, pronounced "ride-ho." Its literal translation is ride or wagon.

The psychological meaning is self-mastery, freedom from imprisonment, and the story "form" in the psyche. Its energy is presence, rhythm, and cosmic cyclical law.

When it appears in divination, it means journey, ordered growth, justice, action, sound advice, or rationality. When reversed, it could mean restlessness, wrongful imprisonment, hypocrisy, control freak, irrationality, injustice, stasis, rigidity, or crisis.

Raidho represents the ordered movement within space and time as it works with human awareness.

It's all about leading by example and understanding that your actions will speak louder than your words. While Ansuz will tell stories, Raidho lives the stories. It shows us our deepest personal journey and our failures in communication. Raidho shows the habitual way that the mind creates stories and connections.

Raidho can be used to see what direction our life is pulling us. We have a compass within us that can be used when using the energy of this rune. Following your love and interests, your greatest dreams and wishes are the best way to understands Raidho's compass of the inner world. When you meditate on Raidho, you can start to see space and time as a personal reality inside of something imposed on you from outside beings. You can also realistically assess your potential and learn new things about limits and physical laws.

< Kenaz

The next rune is Kenaz, and its literal meaning is "torch."

Its psychological meaning is humility, cognitive faculties, clarity of through, and observation. Its energy is illumination, teaching-learning dynamic, transformation, and controlled energy.

When Kenaz appears in divination, it can mean new information, offspring, transformation, craft, technical or artistic ability. If it appears reversed, it could mean over-conceptualization, elitism, arrogance, ignorance, lack of creativity, inability, breakup, decay, and disease.

Kenaz represents the harnessing and control of fire to be used for illumination and warmth. It shows that we have harnessed energies and forces that are bigger than ourselves. Thurisaz is all about creating tools; Kenaz speaks to the use of tools. It shows us the mystery of change and the ability to make things like nature does.

Ancestrally, we must have our own torches and create our own path of light that eliminates the darkness. Our torches will never extinguish, and they are able to be used to help navigate our ancestral stream and to gain more tools and knowledge from our ancestors that are shown in Ansuz that are ours to use.

X Gebo

The next rune is Gebo, pronounced "gay-boo." Its literal meaning is gift.

The psychological aspects are appreciation, forgiveness, and gratitude. Its energy is the dissolution of barriers through gifting, sacrifice, and exchanged powers.

When it appears in divination, it could mean divine vision, sacrifice, honor, magical exchange, gift, and generosity. While it cannot appear reversed, depending on the other runes in that appear, it could also mean dishonesty, unbalanced behavior, over-sacrifice, dependence, loneliness, greed, or influence-buying.

Gebo is the rune that is surrounded by the most lore. When people say X-mas, the x represents this rune even though most don't realize it. In the Havamal, the Cosmic Law of Compensation is written as "Better not to over-pledge as a gift demands a gift," as well as, "Not man is so generous he will jib at accepting a gift in return for a gift."

Gebo is deeply connected to the exchange of sexual energies between females and males and governs the mystical union, sex magic, and sacred oaths of marriage. The mysteries of Ehwaz will provide you with more information about sacred marriage.

ᚹ Wunjo

The last rune this section is Wunjo, pronounced won-joe. Its literal translation is joy.

Its psychological meaning is shared identity, wishful thinking, like-mindedness, optimism, and contentment. Its energy is genuine friendship, wishing, fulfillment, fellowship, effortless ease, and harmony of like forces.

When it appears in divinations, it could mean prosperity, accomplishment, fellowship, harmony, or joy. If it appears reversed, it could mean betrayal, deception, the blindness of danger, warns of caution, alienation, strife, sorrow, or stultification.

Wunjo is that need to realize all of the soul's will to reach the perfection of the consciousness and then the willpower and drive you to need to realize this during your life. It helps to ward off sorrow and woe so that the multiverse's abundant gifts can easily be bestowed upon you. Wunjo is where you find harmonious energy in functional families, group affiliations, healthy nations, and the world.

Hagal's Aett

ᚺ Hagalaz

The first rune in the second aett is Hagalaz, pronounced hag-all-az. Its literal translation means hail or hailstone.

The psychological meaning is personal past, change, and disruption. Its energy is chaos, destructive natural forces, objective confrontation, seed formation, perfect pattern, power beyond human ability to harness.

If Hagalaz appears in divination, it could mean an inner harmony, completion, corrections, controlled crisis, changes for the long-term good, change according to ideals. Hagalaz cannot appear reversed, but if it appears with certain runes, it could mean blame, obsession with the past, victim-consciousness, short-term disappointment, loss of property, loss of power, stagnation, crisis, or catastrophe.

Hagalaz shows us that there is a big energy change as the Elder Futhark starts its second row of aetts. Hagalaz symbolizes confronting your past patterns. It helps you to find the vast energy flow through and around the human energy system. This is a very impersonal rune, and it shows the power that is typically beyond what humans can harness.

Since it is the ninth rune, it has a special place in the rune ordering because nine has a big significance in the Elder Futhark. Nine represents the completion of a pattern. Nine months is a common human cycle, which is the gestational period for a baby. This is why the rune is protective and can help us to accept the unalterable, and find patience and shelter while things blow over.

ᚾ Nauthiz

The next rune is Nauthiz, pronounced not-this. Its literal translation is the need for the fire of necessity.

Its psychological meaning is effort, need, and resistance. Its energy is urgency, coming forth into being, and necessity.

If this rune appears in divination, it could mean achievement through effort, personal development and life lessons, need-fire or self-reliance, innovation, recognition of your ultimate truth, or resistance. While Nauthiz can't appear reversed, it can sometimes mean unrecognized needs, moral cowardice, guilt, worry, warnings, laxity, drudgery, toil, distress, or constraint of freedom when it appears with certain other runes.

If there was no resistance, then the form would fall apart. We understand that the basic law of motion is that "every action has an equal and opposite reaction." This is where resistance to the unconscious forces show up against new consciousness, but as well as the need to evolve consciousness.

ᛁ Isa

The next rune is Isa, pronounced is-ah. Its literal meaning is ice.

The psychological meaning is self-identity and self-image, ego, focus, and mental faculties. Its energy is stasis, contraction, and stillness.

If Isa shows up in divination, it could mean the unity of being, self-control, ego-consciousness, or concentrated self. While it can't appear reversed, if it in the reading with certain other runes, it could mean psychopathy, lack of change, self-centeredness, immobility, dissipation, blindness, dullness, or egomania

Ice is a beautiful yet treacherous thing. It can lull the traveler to sleep with its serenity and peace. Ice is able to lock life under it and prevent it from moving. However, there is nothing else out there that is as powerful as the graceful movement of a glacier, which can tear apart bedrock as it moves. While ice will typically show itself for what it is, with a bit of glamour, there is nothing more dangerous than a weak area in the ice that can swallow up the unexpecting bystander, leaving behind no trace of what was there.

It is a control rune. As the ego-self begins to strengthen through your spiritual training and thinking, this starts to mature into the new individual you. There is also a darker side of the go as you can see Isa's dark side.

ᛃ Jera

The next rune is Jera, pronounced yehr-ah. Its literal meaning is a year.

If Jera appears in divination, it means timing, proper, peace, plenty, and reward for positive action. In certain readings, it may mean regression, conflict, poverty, bad timing, or repetition.

The harvest during the summer is meant to be winter food, and the seeds from those crops became the next year's summer crops. Attentiveness to the cultivation of our present life is important, but you should lay down the wisdom for the future self.

The movement of the seasons aren't so much connected to time, but with the outflow and inflow of the breath. The rhythms of the breath, heartbeat, dawn, and dusk, and sleep are all the keys to finding Jera's subtle nature. Similar to Isa, Jera is unstoppable energy; it is gradual but is unrelenting; it is indifferent to the human influence and unhurried but persistent.

Jera is focused on the right timing. It is the embodiment of "This too shall pass." When you use this rune, it will help you to understand the mysteries of time and the importance of the psyche to manage and divide time. Deadlines will allow you to do the best and will help you to find motivation and grow to levels beyond where you are. It will help to move us towards doing something when it is the right time.

ᛇ Eihawaz or Ihwaz

The next rune is Ihwaz, pronounced yew-was. Its literal meaning is yew.

The psychological meaning is kundalini, the timeless, and death mysteries. Its energy is the chakra system, immortality, encoding, secrecy, and an axis of heaven-earth-hell.

If Ihwaz appears in divination, it could mean protection, initiation, endurance, and movement toward enlightenment. If it appears reversed, it could mean death, weakness, dissatisfaction, destruction, or confusion.

Eihawaz is the vertical axis of Jera's horizontal axis. It represents the vertical nature and energy of the spine. The spine has 24 vertebrae, which is the same number of runes in the Elder Futhark.

ᛈ Perthro

The next rune in this section is Perthro, pronounced Per-throw. Its literal meaning is unknown.

Its psychological meaning is prophecy, recognizing patterns, magic and art of guessing, living with unknown, and coincidence. Its energy is the unmanifest, the unborn, nothingness, luck, and evolutionary force.

If Perthro appears in divinations, it could mean evolutionary change, joy, fellowship, knowledge of orlog, and good omens. If it looks reversed, it could mean unknowability, fantasy, delusion, loneliness, stagnation, emotional or psychological addictions, or doom.

It's important to remember Perthro's true meaning isn't known to scholars since it isn't a recognized word. While plenty of people have said it means "lot cup." I think that "nameless" or "unknown" is more significant.

Perthro is representative of orlog, which is a concept of the matrix of cause and effect. It covers the unalterable and the fixed law of reaction and action. Wyrd words outside of your cause and effect. It isn't fixed like orlog is. Anyone can move around inside their own wyrd according to how developed they are.

ᛉ Algiz

The next rune in this section is Algiz, pronounced Al-jiz. Its literal translation is elk.

Its psychological meaning is a state of listening, higher self, and divinity. Its energy is Valkyries, the divine plan, protective teaching force.

If Algiz appears in divinations, it could mean protection, higher life, awakenings, or connection to the gods. If it looks reversed, it could mean fear, loss of divine link, consumption by divine forces, or hidden dangers.

Algiz is the strongest energy that is connected to existence. This force teaches and promotes autonomy and independence, along with faith. Courage, when faced with fear, is fundamental and not having a total absence of fear since fear might or might not be a warning that you need some sort of defense or protection. Algiz provides you with the insight that you need to make the right decision and to stand in service to Asgard.

ᛊ Sowilo

The last rune in this section is Sowilo, pronounced So-ilol. Its literal translation is the sun.

Its psychological meaning is wholeness, revelation, the seat of the soul, and central nervous system. Its energy is action, life-giving force, motivation, cosmic energies, strengthens the charkas, and sun-wheel.

If Sowilo appears in divinations, it could mean faith in outcomes, life purpose, honor, goals, success, hope, guidance. This rune can't be reversed, but if it looks like it is or appears with other runes, it could mean loss of goals, gullibility, false success, bad advice, and false goals.

The Sowilo is the sun's rune. It's the opposite force of the ice with Isa. It shows us the fire's force within the mental and physical world. It can help to promote persistence, dedication, optimism, and invigoration for anything you want to do. It wards off other people's harmful opinions to keep the heart focused.

It holds a code of honor. All of the guidelines are common sense, and the morality in them is what holds our society together beyond what law can make a person do. Sowilo is all about victory and success. It has been associated with Tiwaz, which will be the next rune we talk about. Sowilo provides you with the power to win and can connect you with revelations about your purpose in life and actions that will guide you in everything you do.

Tyr's Aett

↑ Tiwaz

The first run in the last Aett is Tiwaz, pronounces "tea-waz." Its literal meaning is the god, Tyr.

Its psychological meaning is righteousness, spiritual warrior, and honor. Its energy is the right decision making, sovereign order, and sacrifice.

When it appears in divination, it means even-handedness, honesty, victory, analysis, self-sacrifice, rationality, justice, loyalty, and faith. When reversed, it means, tyranny, defeat, imbalance, injustice, over-sacrifice, over-analysis, or mental paralysis.

Tiwaz is seen as a warrior rune because of Tyr, the god of law and justice. Tyr is a one-handed god and has a very colorful history. He sacrificed one of his hands to trick the wolf, Fenris, into being chained.

Tiwaz will help to correct the balance of the scales so that you know there is going to be a fair decision and hearing. Don't allow the chaos of the environment to throw you off balance. Like the North star, you need to stay calm and true.

ᛒ Berkano

The next rune is Berkano, pronounced "Burr-can-oh." Its literal translation is a birch goddess.

Its psychological meaning is dependence, mature wisdom, safety, silence, and secrecy. Its energy is plant life, trees, female fertility, and releaser.

When it appears in divination, it means, secrets, sanctuary, liberation, shelter, life changes, becoming, and birth. If reversed, it means insecurity, conspiracy, stagnation, sterility, deceit, and the blurring of consciousness.

Berkano contains the power of a birch grove, and this can serve as a safe place in times of need. This is the first tree to come to life during the spring, and as such, Berkano is the cyclical nature of life. This rune is all about maternity and shows the womb ready for child-bearing. It also represents protection and concealment of what is coming together.

ᛖ Ehwaz

The next rune is Ehwaz, pronounced "eh-was." Its literal translation is horse.

Its psychological meaning is sexuality and trust between individual beings. Its energy is cooperation and trust.

When it shows up in divination, it means friends, loyalty, marriage, trust, teamwork, and harmony. If it is reversed, it means an enemy, indecision, nightmares, betrayal, mistrust, disharmony, and duplication.

Ehwaz symbolizes the different vessels as vehicles for movement and travel. Twins are symbolic of the Sacred Marriage of the outer and inner, or body and mind. A horse and ride are some of the best ways to show the symbiotic relationship between two people.

Ehwaz is not about force, but cooperation, suggestion, and persuasion. The dependence, loyalty, and trust built between two people will create a spiritual and emotional connection.

ᛗ Mannaz

The next rune is Mannaz, pronounced "man-az." Its literal meaning is mankind.

Its psychological meaning is perfected intelligence, rational mind, development of the intellect, the difference between humans and other life, and mind and memory. Its energy is the projection of self into time, and the psychic order of the gods.

When it appears in divination, it means divine influence in life, social order, awareness, intelligence, sustainability, and divine structure. When reversed, it means intellectual arrogance, elitism, bigotry, collective suicide, self-delusion, blindness, mortality, and depression.

Every human can reach the state of the perfected human, no matter their name or race. Access to the whole unconscious collection of humanity and earth can be found through Mannaz. It holds answers to some of life's deepest mysteries. It is the rune of human intelligence and rational mind. It is helpful for academic success, contests, and tests.

ᛚ Laguz

The next rune is Lagus, pronounced "log-uhz." It's literal translation is water or ocean.

Its psychological meaning is dreaming, love, unconscious mental processes, psychic powers, and emotion. Its energy is evolution, love as unity, the astral plane, collective unconscious, origins of life, ocean spirit, and life energy.

If it appears in divination, it means dreams, memory, unconscious growth, the sea of vitality, passing a test, and life. If reverse, it means, toxicity, poison, fantasy, lack of moral fiber, emotional blackmail, manipulations, depression, withering, avoidance, circular motion, or fear.

Water symbolizes invisible life forces. Life depends on water, and so Laguz is our universal ocean. Laguz is present in everything and underlies all manifestation. It can be used to establish a communication link between the conscious mind, willful intent, and the unconscious mind.

◇ Inguz

The next rune if Inguz, pronounces "ing-guz." Its literal meaning is seed or the god, Ing.

Its psychological meaning is wholeness, inner-child, power of suggestion, personal development, and internal growth. Its energy is planned bursts, subtlety, male mysteries, gestation process, stored energy, and earth-god.

When it appears in divination, it means time for oneself, expectation, internal growth, gestation, or resting. When reversed, it means immaturity, frivolity, movement without change, scattering, or impotence.

Inguz is the potential energy that has to accumulate slowly in storage before it can be released in one burst of energy. It is the process of a mental seed that is created by the conscious mind into the subconscious for gestation, later to show up as a creation in your life.

ᛞ Dagaz

The next rune is Dagaz, pronounced "day-gahz." Its literal meaning is day or dawn.

Its psychological meaning is satori, enlightenment, conceptual realization, incommunicable experience, and paradoxical truth. Its energy is transmutation, synthesis, unity, non-dual reality, and dawn polarity.

When it appears in divination, it means paradigm shift, the ideal, hope-happiness, awareness, or awakening. If reversed, it means cataclysmic change, hopelessness, blindness, sleep, or lack of vision.

Dagaz works as the opposite of Jera. They both deal with time. Jera is an annual cycle, whereas Dagaz is a daily cycle. They both represent change. Jera is gentle, but Dagaz is a bold change, like a moment of realization.

ᛟ Othala

The very last rune is Othala, pronounced "oh-thall-ah." Its literal translation is an ancestral lot or homeland.

Its psychological meaning is ancestral spiritual power. Its energy is a utopia, paradise, the gift of Ing, heaven on earth, and inheritance.

In divination, it means productive interaction, freedom, group order, group prosperity, or home. When reversed, it means genocide, racism, xenophobia, homelessness, poverty, slavery, totalitarianism, or lack of customary order.

Othala takes care of the matters of ancestry, inheritance, estate, and family. Othala and Fehu are runes of wealth, and they continue the cyclical nature of the runes, simply by the fact that they are the first and last rune.

Chapter 3:

Divination With Runes

In the ancient Germanic worldview, the spoken word holds a lot of creative powers. Catharina Raudvere, a Scandinavian scholar, said that pronouncing words was seen as having a lot of influence over life. The impact that a spoken sentence had couldn't be questioned and was never able to be taken back as if it were physical in some way. They believed words were able to create reality and not the other way around. Germanic society believed that if you spoke a thought out loud, you were making the thought a reality, altering all reality accordingly.

Each rune is a phoneme. This is the smallest sound unit in language, like "r," "t," or "s." For today's linguists, they often forget that there is a connection between the signified, the world's reality, and the signifier. The sound that you use to say the world is simply arbitrary. But there are some linguists who embrace an opposing theory, which is referred to as "phonosemantics." This is the thought that there is a connection between the sounds of a word and what the word means. Basically, this means the phoneme carries a meaning.

This view of language agrees with what Northern European's believed. Runes create the inherent creative power of speech as a visual medium. Besides the fact that rune means letter second to mystery or secret, we need to remember the ordeal that Odin had to go through to discover these runes.

When looking at the runes through a phonosemantic perspective, it takes on another layer of significance. It shows that the relationship between the graphic representation and phoneme in meaningful. This means that the runes weren't just a means of fostering communication. They could also facilitate communication between the invisible world and the visible world, which provided them the basis for a plethora of magical acts.

Runes have been used to write several different languages, which include Hebrew, Russian, Lithuanian, Icelandic, Norwegian, Swedish, Danish, English, Frisian, German, Gothic, and other Semitic languages. Runes are able to be read from left to right or right to left, even on a single artifact. This means that it is very hard to translate a runic inscription, and it is further complicated by the fact that runemasters would sometimes write cryptic puzzles.

Reading Runes

Runes are commonly used for divination purposes. They can be used in order to find guidance through issues or problems and to help shine a light on what your problem is. They are not meant to be used as fortune-tellers, and you will never receive a direct or exact answer. Instead, they provide you with possible options and will suggest ways on how you should act should something happen. Runes will normally hint at answers, but they leave the details up for interpretation, which is where you will need to trust your intuition.

Runic readers understand that our future is not set in stone and that everybody can follow whatever path they want, and can change the future. This means that if you don't really agree with what the runes say, then you have the chance to change your direction, path, or change your route completely.

You can use runes in many different situations. For example, a situation that could be helpful to ask the runes about is if you have something coming up where you don't have a lot to go on, or you can only get an incomplete picture of what is going on.

When you do cast runes, you aren't fortune-telling. The idea behind reading is you ask or think about a question or issue, and then the unconscious and conscious minds work together. Once the runes are cast before you, they aren't random but are arranged by the choices that you made through your subconscious.

As far as what you can ask runes, some people will tell you that you need to focus only on issues you have questions about, but others say you can ask any type of question. No matter which method you use, you need to make sure that you keep your issue or question clear in your mind as you cast the runes.

Remember, you aren't going to get any definitive answers. You are trying to find possible cause and effect and potential outcomes.

As far as what runes you should use, you can purchase rune sets in many different materials, include metal, bone, crystal, stone, or wood. You don't have to have anything fancy when you first start out. The more accustomed you get to runes and reading them, feel free to get a special set. For example, if there is a particular crystal you are drawn to, you can purchase a rune set in that particular crystal. You can even make your own runes if you would like.

No matter what you choose, the material you choose for your runes is very personal. Every rune set will come with a booklet that explains the runes, its symbols representation, and how to interpret it.

Just like with any type of oracle or divination readings, it takes a bit of time to master the actual reading process. You can find lots of guides and books to help you understand their meanings, like the last chapter, and how they affect your life and the question you are asking. It also helps if you are already well in tune with your intuition because it can help you to interpret the meaning. Don't worry, though, if at first, you feel unsure. Persevere, and write down all of your readings.

Starting Your Reading

To start your rune reading, you will need to find a quiet place and take a few minutes to sit in meditation so that you can clear your mind and get yourself focused on what you want to ask the runes. Think about your questions or issue, and if you want, you can call upon your spirit guides or pray to help guide you through the reading.

Spread your rune cloth in front of you to get ready for your casting. There are many different types of casting that you can do, which are a lot like tarot layouts, but with your first reading, you may just want to pick out a single rune and analyze how it applies to your question.

This is a helpful method if you are feeling a bit uncertain or unsure. Picking one rune might provide you with a bit of focus. Once you feel you have gotten the hang of reading a single rune, you can move onto some of these other layouts and casts.

Single Stone Reading

This reading is a simple version that takes just one stone to do a reading. You need to put all your runes in one bag. Here is what you need to do:

Focus and clear your mind. Know the question you want to answer. Keep the bag in your receptive hand. Shake the runes around with your receptive hand to make the stones up. However, you would like to ask your question, do it now.

Reach into the bag and take out one stone. Read the symbol on the stone. This is the answer to your question. If you need more clarification, take one more stone from the bag and read it. If you still need clarification, put the stones back into the bag and mix them up again. Try to rephrase your question, so the spirits understand it better.

When you have reached a comfort level working with runes, you can experiment with various layouts that naturally come to you as you get more advanced in your readings. By doing this, you can find the ways that will work best for you.

Three Rune Layout

This is a good beginner's layout. Get yourself ready as we went over in the last section, and then you will randomly choose three runes out of the bag and place them out in front of you.

The first rune will go on the right, the second in the middle, and the third on the left. When looking at them, they will be laid out as 3, 2, 1.

With this reading, the first rune is showing an overview of your question or situation.

The second rune shows you what your challenge is.

The third rune shows you the possible course of action that you could take.

Four Stone Layout

This reading is more complicated and would be best left for people how to have an advanced understanding of rune stones. This type of reading makes you read four different stones. Here is what you need to do:

Focus and clear your mind. Know what question you would like answers to. Hold your rune bag with your receptive hand. Using the fingers on your receptive hand, mix the stones around in the bag. However, you want to ask your question, do it now.

Reach into the bag and pick one stone. Continue doing this until you have four stones. Read the symbol of the stone. The very first stone represents the influence that your past has on you. The second is the influences that your present has. The third is the influence of your future. The fourth is all about the energies and behaviors that will remain the same.

Five Rune Layout

With a five rune cast, you will pick out a single rune at a time and lay them out on your cloth in a certain place.

Your first rune should be placed in the middle, and the other four will create a cross around it. The second rune will be placed on the left side of the center rune, the third rune goes at the top, the fourth at the bottom, and the fifth at the right. You have the choice of laying them out face up, or you can place them face down and then flip them over when you are ready to read them.

The basis of this layout is that the three runes that run horizontally, rune numbers two, one, and five, show you the past, present, and future. The very bottom rune shows what about your situation or problem that you need to accept, and the very top rune represents the things that could help you in relation to the issue.

Nine Rune Layout

For the Norse people, the number nine is magical, so this is a favorite casting among experienced runemasters. This is a great option if you want to figure out where you are along your path and what you should do next. This is also a cast that helps to test your intuition.

To do this casting, give some thought to your spiritual needs and choose nine runes, and then hold them in your hand for a few moments. The scatter then over your cloth.

Typically, runes that fall closer to the center of the cloth relate most to the situation at hand, your present, so to speak. That means the ones that land closer to the edges aren't as important. If there are runes that are rather close to one another or are touching, they could be complementing influences. But, if there are two runes at opposite sides of your cloth, then they show opposing influences.

You need to focus on the runes that landed face-up, first. It may be a good idea to write those down so that you can look them up and study them a bit more. Once you are done with the face-up rune, you can start to turn over the ones that landed upside down, making sure you live them where they landed. These upside-down runes represent future or outside influences that may show you some new possibilities.

When you are interpreting your runes, make sure that you put your intuition to good use. This is a rune casting where you don't have any set rules, and it is all up to you and your interpretation.

Midgard Serpent Layout

This is a more advanced layout. The Midgard Serpent is supposedly a beast who lives in the sea around the world and is so long that it can bite its own tail. With this layout, we take into consideration that the serpent is able to bite its own tail, and it is very important that you are aware of this fact when interpreting your reading because if you're not careful, the results could pass you by.

Most people will lay out the seven runes in a flowing manner, but the pattern is not as important. The line in which your place the runes gives you a better understanding of their meanings. You can pretend that you are starting out at the first spot, the tail, and then walking along the line until you get to the head of the serpent. While you are making this journey, you will face uphill journeys, which are obstacles that you have to overcome, and downhill journeys, which are times after you have conquered the obstacle.

Just like we did in the other readings, you will center your mind and come up with the question you have for the runes. You will slowly set out seven runes, from left to right. Then you will interpret them

The first rune represents your feelings in the distant past in relation to what your question or situation is that you need help with.

The second rune shows your struggles with your problem as a result of your feelings that the first rune discussed. This "hump" shows use the obstacles that you might have overcome, and you need to be aware of how you handled them before because it could come back again in the present.

The third rune shows your feelings or concerns about the problem presently. Physically, it is the closest rune, so it doesn't just show the present, but the close connection to your feelings.

The fourth rune shows you where the start of the journey towards an outcome. The obstacles you might have had before can come back into play. This hill is steeper, which could mean that the obstacles can be harder to work through. However, you do have your past experiences with this to help guide you.

The fifth rune shows that you have reached the peak of your journey, and you can start to see the goal more clearly. This will show you your feelings and how they end up controlling you once you think you can achieve the goal. You can't let those feelings get the better of you; instead, you need to learn that you need those feelings to reach your goal but also don't let them control you.

The sixth run will remind you that you have work to do to reach your goal if you really want it.

Take this to heart. If it says that you need to work hard to reach your goal, then that's what you should do. If it has to do with control and power, you might have to be strong and control your emotions.

The last rune represents the head of the serpent. Most of the time, this is going to be your goal. However, since the serpent can bite its own tail, if you don't watch the other runes and what they say, you could end up passing right by your goal and started back over at the tail.

Egil's Whalebone Layout

This casting will work a bit differently than that the other readings. Instead of each rune being interpreted on its own, you will break this 12 rune layout into groups of three positions. For each of the groups, you take the three runes and read than like they were "speaking" to you as a whole. It's a lot like do a three-rune reading, and at the end of the reading, you look at what all three runes are trying to tell you.

The four groups get their name from a book called *Egils Saga Skallagrimssonar*. You don't have to have read the book to be able to understand the layout.

When you layout the runes, you will create two rows. Runes one through are on the top, and runes seven through 12 will be placed right below them.

Runes 1, 2, and 3 are known as Carver's Intentions. In the book, the first rune carver had come up with a specific intention for what he would like his runes to do. This group acts the same for you during your cast. You are consulting your runes because you have an intention, situation, or goal. Before you perform this cast, you will need to figure out what you want to learn from the runes. You need to remember what this is throughout the rest of your reading. These first threes tell you how the runes feel about your intentions. You have to notice what you say in your mind as you work towards your goal.

Runes 4, 5, and 6 are known as Helga's Results. Helga gets hurt in the story because of wrongfully carved runes. For this set of runes, it lets you see the possible "negative" results that you could experience if your intention isn't pure or you aren't willing to put the work in to reach the goal.

Runes 7, 8, and 9 are known as Thorfinn's Concerns. Thorfinn is Helga's father, and we see that he is worried about his daughter as she lays sick in bed. This rune set shows any outside obstacles or concerns that could come into play as you work towards your goal. Outside influence can do one of two things for you. One is that they could support you and help you to reach what you want. Second could be that outside influences could hinder you from reaching your goals. The runes will let you know what to keep an eye out for.

Runes 10, 11, and 12 are known as Egil's Results. Egil is the runemaster. Despite the fact that he wrongly carved the runes, their results, and the concern of Thorfinn, Egil was able to make things right. It is through is rune skills that this was possible. He could remove the runes from the whalebone and carve new ones, and then make things right once more. While you don't have to carve something into whalebone, you are facing a rune layout. You shouldn't need to cast the runes again to get the results you want. You should only have to look at this group to guide you. Despite all of the other groups, and what they said, this set will tell you how you can overcome all that you have learned and still reach your goals. This doesn't mean you should just ignore the other groups and just follow this one. This last group only tells you how you can reach your goal while also remembering the possible problems of the other groups.

Odin's Nine Layout

When you are laying out your runes for this spread, placed one down and then two right above it. Then three will be placed to the right of these two and then four placed above three. You will do this for five and six, and then place seven, eight, and nine at the end with seven on the bottom and nine on the top.

The first two runes are representative of the past factors that have acted on your questions. One is the hidden influences that happened in the past. Two is your present attitude about these past events.

For the column of three and four, it shows your present forces concerning your question. Three are the hidden influences that are taking place now. Four is your attitude about your present events.

For the column of five and six, it shows you the outcome of your question. Five tells you the hidden influences, obstacles, or delays that could prevent you from getting what you want. Six shows you how you will respond to the result.

The last column shows the power that you have to face the other three columns. Seven tells you that powers you need to overcome the first column. Eight tells you what power you will need to overcome the second column. Nine tells you what power you will need to deal with the third column.

Chapter 4:

Rune Magic

Many people think that runes are only used as a source of divination that originated with the Norse people in Europe. Using runes for divination is just one portion of what rune magic totally encompasses. If you want to know more about how to use runes in your daily life, rituals, and magic, keep reading.

Simple Magic Using Runes

Runes are very dynamic and multi-dimensional in several ways. Once you get to know your runes on a spiritual, deep level, they kind of make their way into your life daily without you even knowing about it. If you are quite to that level yet, or you need some new ideas, here are some ways to use runes in your daily life:

- Place a rune in your pocket to draw in its energy during your day.

- Make a grid using runes. You do this just like you would a crystal grid, but you will use your runes. Keep the grid on your altar or a place where you can see it.
- Wear jewelry that has been inscribed with your favorite rune.
- Try writing your name using runes.
- Write an affirmation with your runes.
- Pull ONE rune stone and meditate on its meaning all day. Write it on your calendar and pick a new one every day for 24 days.
- Talk a walk in nature and listen for the runes to speak to you through nature. I have taken walks and seen Kenaz in the clouds, Algiz spray-painted on the side of a building, or Elwaz in a fallen twig, etc. You might be surprised just how many runes you will see once you are open-minded enough and willing to receive them.
- When you wake up each morning, do a stadha. These are similar to sun salutations in yoga.

- Anytime you do a blessing or cleansing in your home, dip your finger into oil and draw a protective rune over your fireplace, windows, doors, etc.
- When you sign your name, end it with your favorite rune. Don't do this on any legal document.
- You can draw runes on your body to help with healing:
    - Berkano if you need general healing
    - Lagus helps with blockages
- Draw runes on your foods with sauces
- While you are cooking, draw runes over your food in the air. You could also draw one over your water, tea, or coffee. Pick a rune for your specific intention.

Rituals Using Runes

Using runes in your ritual can bring added power. Runes are wonderful to use with candle magic. You just inscribe the rune into the candle for more intention and power. Draw the rune by using natural items like flowers, twigs, or rocks in the center of your circle or altar. You will need to pick runes that have meanings for your intention. You need to be picky here. Don't just pick something randomly. Allow their personality to speak to you and ask them to bring their energy into your ritual. Here are some more ways to add runes to your rituals:

- Draw runes on your face and body using ritual paint before you begin your ritual and during the ritual to bring the runes' forces.
- Draw runes in the earth in the center of your circle if you are doing a ritual outside.
- Paint or carve runes onto your athames, staffs, staves, wands, etc.
- Draw power and protective runes in the air as you cast your circle before and after your rituals.
- Paint bind runes, place them in a frame, and hang them above your sacred place or altar.
- If you are able to go into a trance, do so. While in the trance craft bind runes for your personal empowerment, to increase your intuition, and to help you communicate with ancestors.

Make Your Own Runes

You want to make your own set of runes, but you don't have any idea how to begin. First let me say that when you make your own set of runes, you will soon realize that your readings will be more accurate. Why? Well, you are putting your energy into the set and filling them with your power, and this can help you with your readings.

When you make your runes, whatever material you decide to use is completely up to you. You can use stones that you have picked up on nature walks. You can cut some small wooden pieces from a tree branch that fell. You could even use clay and bake them. The choices are yours. I will discuss the methods that I have used and how I made them. Later I will show you ways to add power to your runes before you use them. Some people call this consecrating the runes. It isn't necessary, but it can help your runes be more personal.

Small Rocks or Stones

The easiest way to make runes is to gather stones or small rocks that are about the same size. Then you grab your favorite color of paint and paint each rune on each rock. If you can't figure out what color you should use, red is always a good choice. It was the color that the rune carvers of the past used. Once you have painted the runes, you might want to seal or coat the rock so the paint won't wear off. You should be able to find a glaze at most hardware stores. If you can't find one, find a store associate and ask them for help. They should be able to tell you where they are and which one will work the best for what you want it for.

Wooden Tiles

If you don't have small rocks or stones near you, or you just want to use something other than rocks, wood is your next best choice. It is very easy to work with, and you can make the tiles into any shape you want. The easiest way to make them is from wood is by cutting them from a fallen branch. Cutting some circular disks is a quick and easy way. Now you get to choose the way you will put the runes onto the wood. You could paint them, use ink, carve them into the wood, or burn them into the wood. When you are finished putting the runes on your wood, you can stain the wood to make it pretty. If you are painting the runes on the wood, you do this after you have stained the wood. If you use ink, burn, or carve the runes, you need to do that before you stain the wood. There aren't any set rules that you have to stain the wood; you could just leave it natural.

Runes From Clay

I haven't actually tried this one because I don't completely understand how to "fire" it after I have created the ruins. If you know of anyone who has a ceramic studio or works with clay, you might be able to ask them for help. There is some clay on the market that will just harden in the air, but I'm not sure how sturdy they will be.

Clay is easy to work with. Just purchase some at your local hobby shop and mold it into whatever shape you want for your runes. Then you carve the symbols into the clay and "fire" them according to the package directions. I haven't tried this way because I don't work with clay, but I'm sure there are other ways you can decorate your runes.

Bone

If you hunt or know of people who hunt that will give you some animal bones, this is one more option for making runes. Some people won't every use bones due to the way they feel about animals. This choice is completely up to you.

Working with bone is hard. If you know somebody who has a bone saw, you can ask them to cut the tiles for you. If not, you might have to purchase a hacksaw at your local hardware store. You might have to ask for some help, and you may get some odd looks when you ask them to help you cut bones. Once you have painted the rune symbols on the bones, you need to seal or coat it so that the paint won't chip just like you did with the rocks. Carving is going to be a bit hard on bone, and I have no idea how you can even do it.

Consecrating the Runes

Once you have made your runes, now you need to consecrate them. This is similar to a dedication, as it will add your power to the runes. If you plan on using the runes for religious rituals, you can design a small ritual and consecrate them just like you have your other tools. If you are using your runes for casting, then you could do the following.

Take your runes, a bowl of water, and a candle. Light the candle and put your runes to the left of the candle. Take one rune and dab your finger into the water. Rub the water onto the rune as you say its name. If you don't have all of them memorized, you can have a piece of paper next to you with all the names on it. Now pas the rune over the flame of the candle and say the name again. Put the rune onto the table to the right of the candle and say its name one more time. Do this with each rune until you have consecrated every one. You can now use your runes.

Making a Rune Charm

I'm not very talented when it comes to crafty things. When I have to make anything, I like to keep it simple. Here is how to make some rune charms:

You are going to need:

- Small crystal chips
- Herbs of choice, pinch
- Red pen or paint
- Small piece of paper
- Glass vial necklace

How to Make the Charm:

- Cleanse all the charm supplies and the vial by passing them through some sage smoke.
- Write or paint your rune in red on the paper
- Sprinkle the herbs on the runes you drew on the paper
- Roll the paper up and place it into the vial. Be careful with the herbs. Make sure they remain inside the paper.
- Add the crystal chips or other charms to your vial
- Place the cork on it
- Wear it wherever you go.

A quick tip, if you need to recharge your charm, place it in the light of the new or full moon. It all depends on your intention.

Making a Runic Talisman

Talismans are just a spell in a jar or a physical version of magic that you can perform. Here is how you can make, charge, and use one.

Talismans like this can be constructed by using various pieces of magic. The runes are mostly used, but other symbols could be used, too. Whoever is making the talisman gets to decide on what the charm will be used for.

Once this has been decided, pick either three, five, seven, or 13 symbols that will support your purpose. For example, if you need a charm to help you with a successful overseas business deal, you could use Algiz, which is the rune for protection, Raido, which is the rune for traveling, or Fehu, which is the rune for wealth.

The hard part of making charms is finding ways to combine all of the symbols into one. This might mean you put one symbol on top of the others or extend one symbol into the next one, or any method that works for you.

If you do this very sloppy or the symbols don't connect right, the charm might not work. There are other properties you might want to think about, and that is rotational and centerline symmetry, but these aren't as important.

When you have your symbol made, pick the medium that you want to inscribe it into. If you choose paper, it will work for one certain situation once you use it.

If you engrave your talisman into stone or wood, it will be a charm that will last for as long as the talisman lasts. You could draw it into dust or sand, and this will last until it is swept up or disturbed.

When you make your talisman, write it once onto a sheet of paper or piece of cloth and once on the material you will be using. When this is done, burn the paper or cloth and keep its ashes.

Sprinkle the ashes onto your talisman. If you want your talisman to be strong, you can use your blood. Just mix a drop of your blood into the dye, ink, or paint that you will be using and trace the symbol one more time after the ashes.

If you are just going to be using the talisman once and you wrote it on paper, it needs to be burned when you want to use it. This can be very powerful because it releases all of the magical energy at one time.

Please think about the best time for you to use your talisman. Permanent talismans will have their effect if they are close to you or you wear them. Think about keeping them close to you as they will have a slower, drawn-out effect.

Conclusion

Thank you for making it through to the end of the book. I hope that the information has been helpful and informative. Runes are a magical thing. They can be used for divination purposes, and they can be used in spells. With the right knowledge and understanding of their meaning, it is possible to use them in just about any way you want.

Hopefully you enjoyed this book, Thank you for reading.

Sebastian Berg